SELECTED POEMS

SELECTED POEMS

By EDGAR A. GUEST

REILLY & LEE
CHICAGO

SELECTED POEMS
By Edgar A. Guest

Printed in U.S.A.

Dedicated to the many, many people whose preference for these verses has caused them to be singled out for publication in this volume of "Selected Poems."

CONTENTS

CONTENTS — Continued

MY CREED

To live as gently as I can;
To be, no matter where, a man;
To take what comes of good or ill
And cling to faith and honor still;
To do my best and let that stand —
The record of my brain and hand;
And then, should failure come to me,
Still work and hope for victory.

To have no secret place wherein
I stoop unseen to shame or sin;
To be the same when I'm alone
As when my every deed is known;
To live undaunted, unafraid
Of any step that I have made;
To be without pretense or sham
Exactly what men think I am.

To leave some simple mark behind
To keep my having lived in mind;
If enmity to aught I show,
To be an honest, generous foe,
To play my little part, nor whine
That greater honors are not mine.
This, I believe, is all I need
For my philosophy and creed.

THROUGHOUT THE YEARS

Throughout the years that we've been wed,
With all their stormy weather
And all their fits of doubt and dread,
Somehow we've kept together.
Somehow, my dear, in spite of care
And hurts that came to smart us
And little wrongs which seemed unfair,
We've never let them part us.

Oh, we've had days of storm and stress,
And we've had griefs that tried us;
But sorrow never made love less
Or threatened to divide us.
Somehow in spite of all I've done
And said when irritated,
We've managed to keep going on
Like sweethearts, newly mated.

We've had our share of ups and downs
And tasks to irk and fret us,
Our foolishness brought frequent frowns,
Our blunders grave upset us.
But since the tie that binds oft snaps
For others just as plucky,
And we've escaped disaster, p'raps,
My dear, we've just been lucky.

BE A FRIEND

Be a friend. You don't need money —
Just a disposition sunny,
Just the wish to help another
Get along some way or other;
Just a kindly hand extended
Out to one who's unbefriended;
Just the will to give or lend —
This will make you someone's friend.

Be a friend. You don't need glory;
Friendship is a simple story.
Pass by trifling errors blindly,
Gaze on honest effort kindly,
Cheer the youth who's bravely trying,
Pity him who's sadly sighing;
Just a little labor spend
On the duties of a friend.

Be a friend. The pay is bigger
(Though not written by a figure)
Than is earned by people clever
In what's merely self-endeavor.
You'll have friends instead of neighbors
For the profits of your labors;
You'll be richer in the end
Than a prince, if you're a friend.

COMPENSATION

I'd like to think when life is done
    That I had filled a needed post,
That here and there I'd paid my fare
    With more than idle talk and boast;
That I had taken gifts divine,
The breath of life and manhood fine,
And tried to use them now and then
In service for my fellow men.

I'd hate to think when life is through
    That I had lived my round of years
A useless kind, that leaves behind
    No record in this vale of tears;
That I had wasted all my days
By treading only selfish ways,
And that this world would be the same
If it had never known my name.

I'd like to think that here and there,
    When I am gone, there shall remain
A happier spot that might have not
    Existed had I toiled for gain;
That some one's cheery voice and smile
Shall prove that I had been worth while;
That I had paid with something fine
My debt to God for life divine.

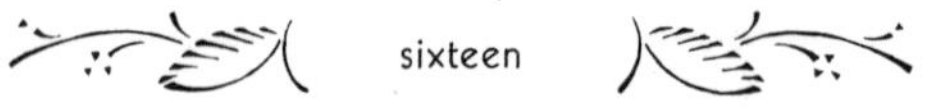

COURAGE

This is courage: to remain
Brave and patient under pain;
Cool and calm and firm to stay
In the presence of dismay;
Not to flinch when foes attack,
Even though you're beaten back;
Still to cling to what is right,
When the wrong possesses might.

This is courage: to be true
To the best men see in you;
To remember, tempest-tossed,
Not to whimper, "All is lost!"
But to battle to the end
While you still have strength to spend;
Not to cry that hope is gone
While you've life to carry on.

This is courage: to endure
Hurt and loss you cannot cure;
Patiently and undismayed,
Facing life still unafraid;
Glad to live and glad to take
Bravely for your children's sake,
Burdens they would have to bear
If you fled and ceased to care.

PRAYER FOR THE HOME

Peace, unto this house, I pray,
Keep terror and despair away;
Shield it from evil and let sin
Never find lodging room within.
May never in these walls be heard
The hateful or accusing word.

Grant that its warm and mellow light
May be to all a beacon bright,
A flaming symbol that shall stir
The beating pulse of him or her
Who finds this door and seems to say,
"Here end the trials of the day."

Hold us together, gentle Lord,
Who sit about this humble board;
May we be spared the cruel fate
Of those whom hatreds separate;
Here let love bind us fast, that we
May know the joys of unity.

Lord, this humble house we'd keep
Sweet with play and calm with sleep.
Help us so that we may give
Beauty to the lives we live.
Let Thy love and let Thy grace
Shine upon our dwelling place.

CHANGE OF MIND

Time was with pride I used to say:
"I hope to leave him rich some day;
I hope he'll never know the cares
Which I have had to bear."
And saying this, it seemed that I
Believed that when I came to die,
My rest would sweeter be to know
My child was free from care.

Today I know parental pride
Was dreaming on its foolish side
And building pictures fair to see,
But bitterly untrue.
Since when have sons to manhood grown
On private incomes of their own?
Since when have sons their merit proved
Without a task to do?

And so no more I shout aloud
From motives filial and proud:
"I want to save my boy from pain
And doubt and loss and care."
No! No! My cry is this today:
"I want to teach my boy the way
To stand to life and work and think
And bravely do his share."

ONLY A DAD

Only a dad with a tired face,
Coming home from the daily race,
Bringing little of gold or fame
To show how well he has played the game;
But glad in his heart that his own rejoice
To see him come and to hear his voice.

Only a dad with a brood of four,
One of ten million men or more
Plodding along in the daily strife,
Bearing the whips and the scorns of life,
With never a whimper of pain or hate,
For the sake of those who at home await.

Only a dad, neither rich nor proud,
Merely one of the surging crowd,
Toiling, striving from day to day,
Facing whatever may come his way,
Silent whenever the harsh condemn,
And bearing it all for the love of them.

Only a dad, but he gives his all
To smooth the way for his children small,
Doing with courage stern and grim
The deeds that his father did for him.
This is the line that for him I pen:
Only a dad, but the best of men.

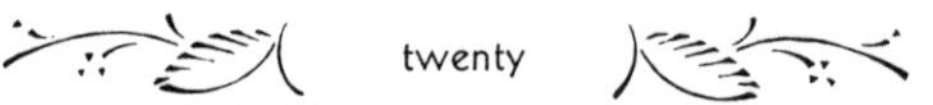

WHEN A BABY ARRIVES

When a little baby comes,
Little fingers, little thumbs,
Little chubby feet and toes
And the little button nose
Give the mother more delight
Than the stars which shine at night.

Others race to get a view
Of that little baby new,
Come the grandmas hastening there
In the happiness to share,
And among the wondering crowd
Walk the grandpas, very proud.

Comes a most devoted aunt,
Whom no other can supplant,
To discover endless charms
In those little dimpled arms
And to bring, as aunties do,
Little gifts of pink or blue.

So in manner quaint and strange,
Thus the lives of many change.
With new hope the future gleams,
New delights, new cares, new dreams,
And with joy the old world hums,
When a little baby comes.

PARENTAL PRIDE

Just a little baby,
    Cute as he can be,
Lovely as the blossom
    On the apple tree.
'Round the wide world over,
    Babies, like the flowers,
Are beautiful to look at,
    But none like this of ours!

There are blue-eyed babies
    Smiling everywhere,
Babes with dimpled elbows,
    Cheeks as soft and fair,
But there's none we'd change for,
    Let the truth be known —
There's no other baby
    As pretty as our own.

Selfish, yes, and boastful,
    Proud as folks can be;
Out of all the babies,
Loveliest is he.
Let the neighbors coldly
    Our conceit discuss,
But God's perfect baby
    Has been sent to us.

BOY OR GIRL

Some folks pray for a boy, and some
For a golden-haired little girl to come.
Some claim to think there is more of joy
Wrapped up in the smile of a little boy,
While others pretend that the silky curls
And plump, pink cheeks of the little girls
Bring more of bliss to the old home place
Than a small boy's queer little freckled face.

Now which is better, I couldn't say
If the Lord should ask me to choose today;
If He should put in a call for me
And say: "Now what shall your order be,
A boy or girl? I have both in store —
Which of the two are you waiting for?"
I'd say with one of my broadest grins:
"Send either one, if it can't be twins."

I've heard it said, to some people's shame,
They cried with grief when a small boy came,
For they wanted a girl. And some folks I know
Who wanted a boy, just took on so
When a girl was sent. But it seems to me
That mothers and fathers should happy be
To think, when the Stork has come and gone,
That the Lord would trust them with either one.

Boy or girl? There can be no choice;
There's something lovely in either voice,
And all that I ask of the Lord to do
Is to see that the mother comes safely through
And guard the baby and have it well,
With a perfect form and a healthy yell,
And a pair of eyes and a shock of hair,
Then, boy or girl — and its dad won't care.

OVER THE CRIB

Over the crib where the baby lies,
Countless beautiful visions rise
Which only the mothers and fathers see,
Visions of splendor that is to be,
Pictures of laughter and joy and song
As the years come sweeping us all along.
Care seldom startles the happy eyes
Over the crib where the baby lies.

A wonderful baby lying there!
And strangers smile at the happy pair,
Proud and boastful, for all they see
Is the dimpled chin and the dimpled knee;
But never a little one comes to earth
That isn't a wonderful babe at birth,
And never a mother who doesn't see
Glorious visions of joy to be.

Over the crib where the baby lies,
Dreams of splendor and pride arise,
Deeds of valor and deeds of love
Hover about and shine above
The tiny form, and the future glows
With a thousand dreams which the mother knows,
And beauty dances before her eyes
Over the crib where the baby lies.

Yet we smile at her and we smile at him,
For we are old and our eyes are dim,
And we have forgotten and don't recall
The visions we saw when our babes were small,
Yet world-wide over the mothers dream,
And ever they see in a golden stream
Wonderful joys in the by-and-by
Over the cribs where their babies lie.

A FRIEND

A friend is one who takes your hand
    And talks a speech you understand;
He's partly kindness, partly mirth,
    And faith unfaltering in your worth;
He's first to cheer you on success,
    And last to leave you in distress;
A friend is constant, honest, true —
    In short, old pal, he's just like YOU!

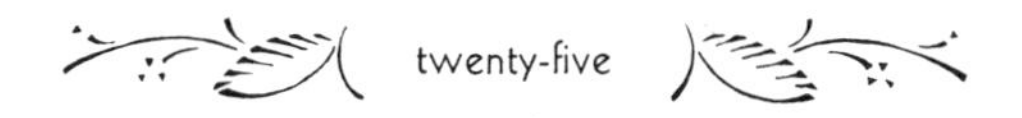

FRIENDSHIP

You do not need a score of men to laugh
and sing with you;
You can be rich in comradeship with just a friend or two.
You do not need a monarch's smile
to light your way along;
Through weal or woe a friend or two
will fill your days with song.

So let the many go their way, and let the throng pass by;
The crowd is but a fickle thing
which hears not when you sigh.
The multitude is quick to run in search of favorites new,
And all that man can hold for grief is just a friend or two.

When winds of failure start to blow,
you'll find the throng has gone —
The splendor of a brighter flame will always lure them on;
But with the ashes of your dreams,
and all you hoped to do,
You'll find that all you really need is just a friend or two.

You cannot know the multitude, however hard you try:
It cannot sit about your hearth; it cannot hear you sigh;
It cannot read the heart of you,
or know the hurts you bear;
Its cheers are all for happy men and not for those in care.

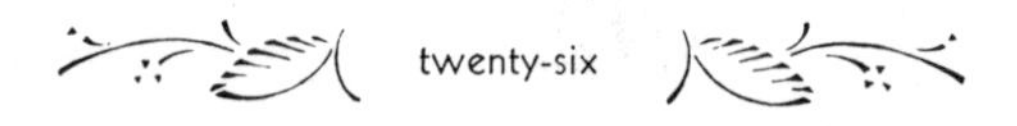

So let the throng go on its way and let the crowd depart;
But one or two will keep the faith
when you are sick at heart;
And rich you'll be, and comforted,
when gray skies hide the blue,
If you can turn and share your grief
with just a friend or two.

A MOTHER FINDS REST

And now she dwells where neither doubt nor fear
May find her breast;
No crying child may now disturb her here
Or break her rest.

Ended the ache of living. Here she lies
In wondrous peace;
God left a smile about her lovely eyes
With her release.

How oft we fretted her or caused her pain,
We cannot say;
Long hours she watched beside the window pane
With us away.

Her sleep we broke with whimpering and sighs
When we were ill;
Nor thought it much to rouse her with our cries,
As children will.

But now we suffer so, and vainly call
For her to come;
Her feet will never tread again the hall,
Her lips are dumb.

Love had no more sweet service to provide,
But this we know:
She'll watch for us upon the other side,
Who tried her so.

I BELIEVE

I believe in friendship, and I believe in trees,
And I believe in hollyhocks a-swaying in the breeze,
And I believe in robins and roses white and red,
And rippling brooks and rivers and blue skies overhead,
And I believe in laughter, and I believe in love,
And I believe the daffodils believe in God above.

I am no unbeliever. I know that men are true,
I know the joy of summer time
when skies above are blue,
I know there is no earthly power
can shape a budding rose,
Or bring a daisy into bloom; with all that wisdom knows
It could not fashion, if it would,
the humblest blade of grass
Or stretch a living carpet where the weary travelers pass.

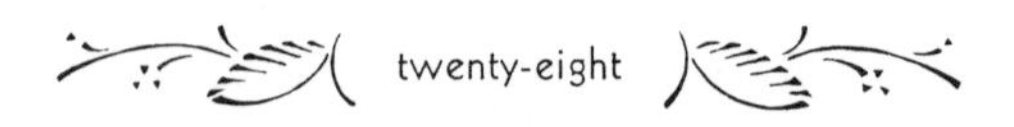

I believe in friendship, for I have found it good,
And I believe in kindly words, for I have understood;
My faith is founded on the years and all that I have seen,
Something of God I've looked upon
no matter where I've been.
Within a swamp but yesterday a lily smiled at me
And only God could set it there to bloom for me to see.

THE MAKING OF FRIENDS

If nobody smiled and nobody cheered
and nobody helped us along,
If each every minute looked after himself
and good things all went to the strong,
If nobody cared just a little for you,
and nobody thought about me,
And we stood all alone to the battle of life,
what a dreary old world it would be!

If there were no such thing as a flag in the sky
as a symbol of comradeship here,
If we lived as the animals live in the woods
with nothing held sacred or dear,
And selfishness ruled us from birth to the end,
and never a neighbor had we,
And never we gave to another in need,
what a dreary old world it would be!

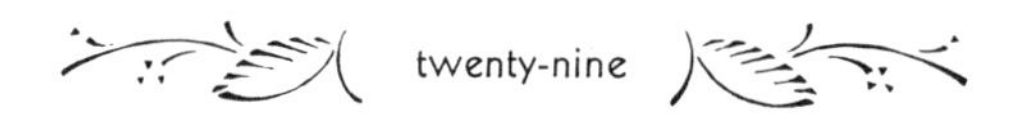

Oh, if we were rich as the richest on earth
and strong as the strongest that lives,
Yet never we knew the delight and the charm
of the smile which the other man gives,
If kindness were never a part of ourselves,
though we owned all the land we could see,
And friendship meant nothing at all to us here,
what a dreary old world it would be!

Life is sweet just because of the friends we have made
and the things which in common we share;
We want to live on not because of ourselves,
but because of the people who care;
It's giving and doing for somebody else,
on that all life's splendor depends,
And the joy of this world, when you've summed it
all up, is found in the making of friends.

A FRIEND LIKE YOU

I want to be a friend like you;
I'd count my life worth while
If I could only learn to do
So much to bring a smile;
I wish that I could grow to be
In all I say and do,
Less like the one folks know as me
And more and more like you!

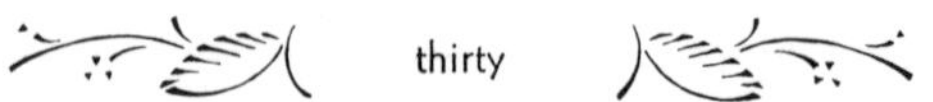

LIFE'S HIGHWAY

'Tis good to walk life's highway wide,
Past cabin low and steeple,
And meet along the countryside
The smiling, friendly people.
For wheresoe'er a man may fare,
Though rough or smooth the mile is,
Or bright the day or dark and gray,
He'll come to where a smile is.

There's sorrow for the hearts of all
Before the journey closes;
But Junetime lines full many a wall
With pink and scarlet roses,
And overhead the blue skies spread
A canopy of splendor
'Neath which we fare, despite our care,
To welcomes warm and tender.

And be the highway short or long
Which stretches out before us,
Man's ear will catch the heartening song
Of thrush or robin chorus.
By stream and brook on scenes he'll look,
Illuming Nature's pages
To glad his eye as he goes by,
Repeated through the ages.

The poorest man a friend may find,
The richest man no truer;
For kings, whom soldiers march behind,
God's sky is made no bluer.
'Spite care and strife, the joys of life,
The beauties richly blended,
And sun and star and blossoms are
For all mankind intended.

MOTHER'S WAY

Tender, gentle, brave and true,
Loving us whate'er we do!
Waiting, watching at the gate
For the footsteps that are late,
Sleepless through the hours of night
Till she knows that we're all right;
Pleased with every word we say —
That is every mother's way.

Others sneer and turn aside,
Mother welcomes us with pride;
Over-boastful of us, too,
Glorying in all we do,
First to praise and last to blame,
Love that always stays the same,
Following us where'er we stray —
That is every mother's way.

She would grant us all we seek,
Give her strength where we are weak,
Beauty? She would let it go
For the joy we yearn to know.
Life? She'd give it gladly, too,
For the dream that we pursue;
She would toil that we might play —
That is every mother's way.

Not enough for her are flowers —
Her life is so blent with ours
That in all we dare and do
She is partner, through and through;
Suffering when we suffer pain,
Happy when we smile again,
Living with us, night and day —
That is every mother's way.

A LOYAL FRIEND

Ain't it good when life seems dreary
　　And your hopes about to end,
Just to feel the handclasp cheery
　　Of a fine and loyal friend?
Ain't it fine when things are going
　　Topsy-turvy and askew,
To discover some one showing
　　Good old-fashioned faith in you?

HOW DO YOU TACKLE YOUR WORK?

How do you tackle your work each day?
Are you scared of the job you find?
Do you grapple the task that comes your way
With a confident, easy mind?
Do you stand right up to the work ahead
Or fearfully pause to view it?
Do you start to toil with a sense of dread
Or feel that you're going to do it?

You can do as much as you think you can,
But you'll never accomplish more;
If you're afraid of yourself, young man,
There's little for you in store.
For failure comes from the inside first,
It's there if we only knew it,
And you can win, though you face the worst,
If you feel that you're going to do it.

Success! It's found in the soul of you
And not in the realm of luck!
The world will furnish the work to do,
But you must provide the pluck.
You can do whatever you think you can,
It's all in the way you view it.
It's all in the start that you make, young man:
You must feel that you're going to do it.

How do you tackle your work each day?
With confidence clear, or dread?
What to yourself do you stop and say
When a new task lies ahead?
What is the thought that is in your mind?
Is fear ever running through it?
If so, just tackle the next you find
By thinking you're going to do it.

LIFE

Life is a gift to be used every day,
Not to be smothered and hidden away;
It isn't a thing to be stored in the chest
Where you gather your keepsakes
and treasure your best;
It isn't a joy to be sipped now and then,
And promptly put back in a dark place again.

Life is a gift that the humblest boast of,
And one that the humblest may well make the most of;
Get out and live it each hour of the day,
Wear it and use it as much as you may;
Don't keep it in niches and corners and grooves —
You'll find that in service its beauty improves.

HOME

It takes a heap o' livin' in a house t' make it home,
A heap o' sun and shadder, an'
ye sometimes have t' roam
Afore ye really 'preciate the things ye lef' behind,
An' hunger fer 'em somehow,
with 'em allus on yer mind.
It don't make any difference how rich ye get t' be,
How much yer chairs an' tables cost,
how great yer luxury;
It ain't home t' ye, though it be the palace of a king,
Until somehow yer soul is sort o' wrapped
'round everything.

Home ain't a place that gold can buy
or get up in a minute;
Afore it's home there's got t' be a heap o' livin' in it;
Within the walls there's got t' be
some babies born, and then
Right there ye've got t' bring 'em up
t' women good, an' men;
And, gradjerly, as time goes on, ye find ye wouldn't part
With anything they ever used —
they've grown into yer heart:
The old high chairs, the playthings, too,
the little shoes they wore
Ye hoard; an' if ye could ye'd keep the thumbmarks
on the door.

Ye've got t' weep t' make it home,
ye've got t' sit an' sigh
An' watch beside a loved one's bed,
an' know that Death is nigh;
An' in the stillness o' the night
t' see Death's angel come,
An' close the eyes o' her that smiled,
an' leave her sweet voice dumb.
Fer these are scenes that grip the heart,
an' when yer tears are dried,
Ye find the home is dearer than it was, an' sanctified;
An' tuggin' at ye always are the pleasant memories
O' her that was an' is no more —
ye can't escape from these.

Ye've got t' sing an' dance fer years,
ye've got t' romp an' play,
An' learn t' love the things ye have
by usin' 'em each day;
Even the roses 'round the porch
must blossom year by year
Afore they 'come a part o' ye, suggestin' someone dear
Who used t' love 'em long ago,
an' trained 'em jes' t' run
The way they do, so's they would get
the early mornin' sun;
Ye've got t' love each brick an' stone
from cellar up t' dome:
It takes a heap o' livin' in a house t' make it home.

THE JUNE COUPLE

She is fair to see and sweet,
Dainty from her head to feet,
Modest, as her blushing shows,
Happy, as her smiles disclose,
And the young man at her side
Nervously attempts to hide
Underneath a visage grim
That the fuss is bothering him.

Pause a moment, happy pair!
This is not the station where
Romance ends, and wooing stops
And the charm from courtship drops;
This is but the outward gate
Where the souls of mortals mate,
But the border of the land
You must travel hand in hand.

You who come to marriage, bring
All your tenderness, and cling
Steadfastly to all the ways
That have marked your wooing days.
You are only starting out
On life's roadways, hedged about
Thick with roses and with tares,
Sweet delights and bitter cares.

disconsolat
that the Christmas se
be held without musi
broken beyond quick
two men had sent for
an organ builder fron
sure he would not a
could they do?

The pastor and th
cided to write a Chris

Rolf Tietgens

Question after Christmas

When fragrant needles dry and spill,
Why pack away the heart's good will
As though it were a specialty
To hang upon the Christmas tree?

Why, when Christmas Day is done,
Do we mortals quickly run
Back into the commonplace?
Where yesterday each passing face
Was eager with a secret chore,
Each holly-hung and ribboned door
Breathed welcome to the passer-by,
Now hurriedly the busy eye
Skims ahead as though good will
Were something Christmas hearts distill,
Then dissipate, as though the air
Could no longer hold it there;
A change as though the very hour
That Christmas ends is like a flower
Which closes when the day departs—
So, too, the closing Christmas hearts
That drop their spent humility
Like needles from the Christmas tree.

Jessie Farnham

Heretofore you've only played
At love's game, young man and maid,
Only known it at its best;
Now you'll have to face its test.
You must prove your love worth while,
Something time cannot defile,
Something neither care nor pain
Can destroy or mar or stain.

You are now about to show
Whether love is real or no;
Yonder down the lane of life
You will find, as man and wife,
Sorrows, disappointments, doubt,
Hope will almost flicker out;
But if rightly you are wed,
Love will linger where you tread.

There are joys that you will share,
Joys to balance every care;
Arm in arm remain, and you
Will not fear the storms that brew,
If when you are sorest tried,
You face your trials side by side.
Now your wooing days are done
And your loving years begun.

THE PATH THAT LEADS TO HOME

The little path that leads to home,
That is the road for me,
I know no finer path to roam,
With finer sights to see.
With thoroughfares the world is lined
That lead to wonders new,
But he who treads them leaves behind
The tender things and true.

Oh, north and south and east and west
The crowded roadways go,
And sweating brow and weary breast
Are all they seem to know.
And mad for pleasure some are bent,
And some are seeking fame,
And some are sick with discontent,
And some are bruised and lame.

Across the world the gleaming steel
Holds out its lure for men,
But no one finds his comfort real
Till he comes home again.
And charted lanes now line the sea
For weary hearts to roam,
But, oh, the finest path to me
Is that which leads to home.

'Tis there I come to laughing eyes
And find a welcome true;
'Tis there all care behind me lies
And joy is ever new.
And, oh, when every day is done
Upon that little street,
A pair of rosy youngsters run
To me with flying feet.

The world with myriad paths is lined
But one alone for me,
One little road where I may find
The charms I want to see.
Though thoroughfares majestic call
The multitude to roam,
I would not leave, to know them all,
The path that leads to home.

I AIN'T DEAD YET

Time was I used to worry an' I'd sit around an' sigh,
An' think with every ache I got that I was goin' to die,
I'd see disaster comin' from a dozen different ways
An' prophesy calamity an' dark an' dreary days.
But I've come to this conclusion,
that it's foolishness to fret;
I've had my share o' sickness, but I
Ain't
Dead
Yet!

Wet springs have come to grieve me
an' I've grumbled at the showers,
But I can't recall a June-time
that forgot to bring the flowers.
I've had my business troubles,
an' looked failure in the face,
But the crashes I expected
seemed to pass right by the place.
So I'm takin' life more calmly,
pleased with everything I get,
An' not over-hurt by losses, 'cause I
Ain't
Dead
Yet!

I've feared a thousand failures
an' a thousand deaths I've died,
I've had this world in ruins by the gloom I've prophesied.
But the sun shines out this mornin'
an' the skies above are blue,
An' with all my griefs an' trouble,
I have somehow lived 'em through.
There may be cares before me,
much like those that I have met;
Death will come some day an' take me, but I
Ain't
Dead
Yet!

A BOY'S TRIBUTE

Prettiest girl I've ever seen
Is Ma,
Lovelier than any queen
Is Ma;
Girls with curls go walking by,
Dainty, graceful, bold and shy,
But the one that takes my eye
Is Ma.

Every girl made into one
Is Ma,
Sweetest girl to look upon
Is Ma;
Seen 'em short and seen 'em tall,
Seen 'em big and seen 'em small,
But the finest one of all
Is Ma.

Best of all the girls on earth
Is Ma,
One that all the rest is worth
Is Ma;
Some have beauty, some have grace,
Some look nice in silk and lace,
But the one that takes first place
Is Ma.

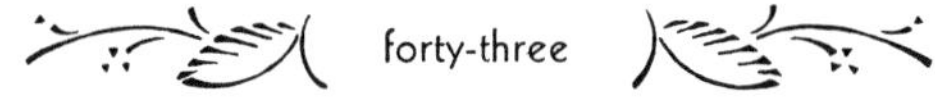

Sweetest singer in the land
Is Ma,
She that has the softest hand
Is Ma;
Tenderest, gentlest nurse is she,
Full of fun as she can be,
And the only girl for me
Is Ma.

Bet if there's an angel here
It's Ma,
If God has a sweetheart dear
It's Ma;
Take the girls that artists draw,
And all the girls I ever saw,
The only one without a flaw
Is Ma.

SOMEBODY CARES

Somebody cares for you,
Cares so much,
That the heart grows glad
At your slightest touch;
And the sound of your voice
And the sight of your smile
Make all my burdens
And cares worth while.

Somebody cares for you —
Bye and bye
When the years roll on,
You will know it's I;
Then, looking back
O'er the road we've fared,
You'll see how much for you
Somebody cared.

EULOGY

This was the way of him, minister, say of him
Only the simplest of praises about him,
Flatter him not today, it is enough to say
Care will be just a bit harder without him.

Friend to us all was he, soonest to call was he
Hearing the word that our hearts were in sorrow;
This is enough to say, now that he's gone away,
Grief will be just a bit harder tomorrow.

Now that he's gone away, we who still living stay,
Missing his smile and his hand at our shoulder,
As the days come and go, 'gainst all the storms that blow,
Stronger we'll have to be, truer and bolder.

A SONG

None knows the day that friends must part,
None knows how near is sorrow;
If there be laughter in your heart,
Don't hold it for tomorrow.
Smile all the smiles you can today;
Grief waits for all along the way.

Today is ours for joy and mirth;
We may be sad tomorrow;
Then let us sing for all we're worth,
Nor give a thought to sorrow.
None knows what lies along the way;
Let's smile what smiles we can today.

A CHRISTMAS BIT

If I were Santa Claus this year,
I'd change his methods for the day;
I'd give to all the children here
But there are things I'd take away.

I'd enter every home to steal,
With giving I'd not be content.
I'd find the heartaches men conceal
And take them with me when I went.

I'd rob the invalid of pain;
    I'd steal the poor man's weight of care;
I'd take the prisoner's ball and chain
    And every crime which sent him there.

I'd take the mother's fears away,
    The doubts which often fret the wise —
And all should wake on Christmas Day
    With happy hearts and shining eyes.

For old and young this is my prayer:
    God bless us all this Christmas Day
And give us strength our tasks to bear,
    And take our bitter griefs away!

WHAT I CALL LIVING

The miser thinks he's living when he's hoarding
    up his gold;
The soldier calls it living when he's doing
    something bold;
The sailor thinks it living to be tossed upon the sea,
And upon this vital subject no two of us agree.
But I hold to the opinion, as I walk my way along,
That living's made of laughter and good-fellowship
    and song.

I wouldn't call it living always to be seeking gold,
To bank all the present gladness for the days
when I'll be old.
I wouldn't call it living to spend all my strength for fame,
And forego the many pleasures which today
are mine to claim.
I wouldn't for the splendor of the world set out to roam,
And forsake my laughing children and the peace
I know at home.

Oh, the thing that I call living isn't gold or fame at all!
It's good-fellowship and sunshine, and it's roses
by the wall;
It's evenings glad with music and a hearth fire
that's ablaze,
And the joys which come to mortals
in a thousand different ways.
It is laughter and contentment and the struggle for a goal;
It is everything that's needful in the shaping of a soul.

MOTHER

Never a sigh for the cares that she bore for me,
Never a thought of the joys that flew by;
Her one regret that she couldn't do more for me,
Thoughtless and selfish, her master was I.

Oh, the long nights that she came at my call to me!
Oh, the soft touch of her hands on my brow!
Oh, the long years that she gave up her all to me!
Oh, how I yearn for her gentleness now!

Slave to her baby! Yes, that was the way of her,
Counting her greatest of services small;
Words cannot tell what this old heart would say of her,
Mother — the sweetest and fairest of all.

THE GOOD WORLD

The Lord must have liked us, I say when I see
The bloom of the rose and the green of the tree,
The flash of the wing of a bird flitting by,
The gold of the grain and the blue of the sky,
The clover below and the tall pines above —
Oh, there's something about us the good Lord must love.

The Lord must have liked us, I say when I stand
Where the waves like an army come into the land,
With the gulls riding high on the crest of the breeze
And the ducks flying north in their echelon V's,
The sun slipping down into liquefied gold —
Oh, it's then the great love of the Lord I behold.

The Lord must have liked us, I say at the dawn
When the diamonds of dew gleam and glow on the lawn,
And the birds from their throats
        pour the red wine of song
As if life held no burden of sorrow or wrong;
The Lord must have loved us, I whisper just then,
To give such a world to the children of men.

The Lord must have liked us, I say as I pass
The nest of a meadow lark deep in the grass,
Or hear in the distance the quail calling clear
And know that his mate and his babies are near;
Oh, I say to myself as His wonders I see,
The Lord loves us all or this never would be.

BOY O' MINE

Boy o' mine, boy o' mine, this is my prayer for you,
This is my dream and my thought and my care for you:
Strong be the spirit which dwells in the breast of you,
Never may folly or shame get the best of you;
You shall be tempted in fancied security,
But make no choice that is stained with impurity.

Boy o' mine, boy o' mine, time shall command of you
Thought from the brain of you,
        work from the hand of you;
Voices of pleasure shall whisper and call to you,

Luring you far from the hard tasks that fall to you;
Then as you're meeting life's bitterest test of men,
God grant you strength to be true as the best of men.

Boy o' mine, boy o' mine, singing your way along,
Cling to your laughter and cheerfully play along;
Kind to your neighbor be, offer your hand to him,
You shall grow great as your heart shall expand to him;
But when for victory sweet you are fighting there,
Know that your record of life you are writing there.

Boy o' mine, boy o' mine, this is my prayer for you:
Never may shame pen one line of despair for you;
Never may conquest or glory mean all to you;
Cling to your honor whatever shall fall to you;
Rather than victory, rather than fame to you,
Choose to be true and let nothing bring shame to you.

OUT FISHIN'

A feller isn't thinkin' mean,
Out fishin';
His thoughts are mostly good an' clean,
Out fishin';
He doesn't knock his fellow men,
Or harbor any grudges then;
A feller's at his finest, when
Out fishin'.

The rich are comrades to the poor,
Out fishin';
All brothers of a common lure,
Out fishin';
The urchin with the pin an' string
Can chum with millionaire an' king;
Vain pride is a forgotten thing,
Out fishin'.

A feller gits a chance to dream,
Out fishin';
He learns the beauties of a stream,
Out fishin';
An' he can wash his soul in air
That isn't foul with selfish care,
An' relish plain an' simple fare,
Out fishin'.

A feller has no time fer hate,
Out fishin';
He isn't eager to be great,
Out fishin';
He isn't thinkin' thoughts of pelf,
Or goods stacked high upon a shelf,
But he is always just himself,
Out fishin'.

A feller's glad to be a friend,
Out fishin';

A helpin' hand he'll always lend,
Out fishin';
The brotherhood of rod an' line
An' sky an' stream is always fine;
Men come real close to God's design,
Out fishin'.

A feller isn't plotting schemes,
Out fishin';
He's only busy with his dreams,
Out fishin';
His livery is a coat of tan;
His creed, to do the best he can;
A feller's always mostly man,
Out fishin'.

HUNGERIN' TO SEE YOU

I'm hungerin' to see you,
As hungry as can be,
Of all the folks in all the world,
It's you I want to see;
I've watched uncounted people
Go smiling on their way,
And some perhaps were friendly

And some were bright and gay;
But they were strange and distant
And passed as strangers do
While my poor heart was hungry —
Just hungerin' for you!

BECOMING A DAD

Old women say that men don't know
The pain through which all mothers go,
And maybe that is true, and yet
I vow I never shall forget
The night he came. I suffered, too,
Those bleak and dreary long hours through;
I paced the floor and mopped my brow
And waited for his glad wee-ow!
I went upstairs and then came down
Because I saw the doctor frown
And knew beyond the slightest doubt
He wished to goodness I'd clear out.

I walked into the yard for air
And back again to hear her there,
And met the nurse, as calm as though
My world was not in deepest woe;
And when I questioned, seeking speech

Of consolation that would reach
Into my soul and strengthen me
For dreary hours that were to be:
"Progressing nicely!" That was all
She said and tiptoed down the hall;
"Progressing nicely!" Nothing more,
And left me there to pace the floor.

And once the nurse came out in haste
For something that had been misplaced,
And I that had been growing bold
Then felt my blood grow icy cold;
And fear's stern chill swept over me,
I stood and watched and tried to see
Just what it was she came to get —
I haven't learned that secret yet.
I half believe that nurse in white
Was adding fuel to my fright
And taking an unholy glee
From time to time, in torturing me.

Then silence! To her room I crept
And was informed the doctor slept!
The doctor slept! Oh, vicious thought,
While she at death's door bravely fought
And suffered untold anguish deep,
The doctor lulled himself to sleep.
I looked and saw him stretched out flat

And could have killed the man for that.
Then morning broke, and oh, the joy,
With dawn there came to us our boy,
And in a glorious little while
I went in there and saw her smile!

I must have looked a human wreck,
My collar wilted at the neck,
My hair awry, my features drawn
With all the suffering I had borne.
She looked at me and softly said:
"If I were you, I'd go to bed."
Hers was the bitterest part, I know;
She traveled through the vale of woe,
But now when women folks recall
The pain and anguish of it all,
I answer them in manner sad:
"It's no cinch to become a dad."

LET'S BE THANKFUL

Thankful for the glory of the old Red, White and Blue,
For the spirit of America that still is staunch and true,
For the laughter of our children
and the sunlight in their eyes,
And the joy of radiant mothers
and their evening lullabies;

And thankful that our harvests wear no taint
of blood today
But were sown and reaped by toilers
who were light of heart and gay.

Thankful for the riches that are ours to claim and keep,
The joy of honest labor and the boon of happy sleep,
For each little family circle where there is no empty chair
Save where God has sent the sorrow
for the loving hearts to bear;
And thankful for the loyal souls
and brave hearts of the past
Who builded that contentment should be with us
to the last.

Thankful for the plenty that our peaceful land
has blessed,
For the rising sun that beckons every man to do his best,
For the goal that lies before him
and the promise when he sows
That his hand shall reap the harvest,
undisturbed by cruel foes;
For the flaming torch of justice, symbolizing as it burns:
Here none may rob the toiler of the prize he fairly earns.

Today our thanks we're giving for the riches that are ours,
For the red fruits of the orchards
and the perfume of the flowers,

For our homes with laughter ringing
    and our hearthfires blazing bright,
For our land of peace and plenty
    and our land of truth and right;
And we're thankful for the glory of the old Red,
    White and Blue,
For the spirit of our fathers and a manhood that is true.

A PRAYER

God grant me kindly thought
    And patience through the day,
And in the things I've wrought,
    Let no man living say
That hate's grim mark has stained
What little joy I've gained.

God keep my nature sweet,
    Teach me to bear a blow,
Disaster and defeat,
    And no resentment show.
If failure must be mine,
Sustain this soul of mine.

God grant me strength to face
    Undaunted day or night;
To stoop to no disgrace
    To win my little fight;
Let me be, when it is o'er,
As manly as before.

Dear Reader:

It is the sincere hope of both author and publisher that you may have found comfort, inspiration and good cheer in the selected poems contained in this little volume.

Perhaps, too, it may have occurred to you, as you read the lines of one especially appealing, that it might bring to others the same solace it brought to you. You may even have had some particular person in mind at the time.

If that should be true, it will doubtless interest you to know that nearly every poem in this volume has been reproduced, individually, in the form of a greeting card or illustrated motto, and can doubtless be obtained from the dealer through whom your volume of "Selected Poems" was secured.

The Publisher